Use You

Learn How to Drive

The Quick and Easy Way to
Pass the Practical Driving Test!

Applicable Worldwide!

Use Your Mind to Learn How to Drive

The Quick and Easy Way to Pass the Practical Driving Test!

Applicable Worldwide!

Martin Woodward

2nd Edition 2015

ISBN: 978-1-326-46779-1

www.martinwoodward.net

Contents

Introduction 3

The Practical Test 5

Your driving ability 6

Your Country of Residence 9

The Test Centre and Area 10

The Date and Time of Day 11

The Test Route 13

Traffic Situations that you may encounter 13

The Weather 14

The Examiner 15

How You Feel on the Day 17

Your Instructor and Car 17

Your Parents and your Childhood 18

Your Spouse / Partner and Friends / Workmates 23

Previous Tests 24

Your Age 24

How Much You Enjoy Driving 25

Your Need to Pass the Test 26

Your Attitude and Confidence 26

Creating the Right Attitude 30

The Zen of Driving *31*

The Vast Power of Your Mind **34**

You Reap What You Sow! *34*

The Universal Subjective / Subconscious Mind *35*

The Law of Reversed Effort *36*

Your Word is Power *37*

You want immediate proof? - Try this! *39*

How conscious are you? *40*

Belief *41*

Technique 1 .... **43**

Step by step *44*

Technique 2 .... **47**

Subliminal, Audible & Bilateral Suggestions *47*

Binaural Beats *48*

Declarations / Suggestions **53**

Ability Analysis Test **57**

The Clutch *58*

Moving Off *70*

Stopping *77*

Clutch Control *81*

Gears *87*

Thank You **97**

Introduction

In 1973 I qualified as a driving instructor and ran my own school in Sheffield. When I sold the school 30 years later (in 2003) it was one of the largest and most successful in South Yorkshire, largely due to my teaching techniques, high pass rate, dedication and attitude. I also worked very long hours for a long time.

During this period I attained the highest instructor grade (6) which is achieved only by a minority of instructors and have personally taught literally thousands of pupils successfully. I've also trained many other instructors, some of whom are still working at the school and others who are working for themselves. I'm not suggesting that I was the best instructor in the world, but clearly I was pretty good and I doubt if anyone anywhere has gained more experience at driving tuition than me.

Over the years I have also studied various *'mind'* techniques and have used them successfully in my personal and business life. This book and accompanying downloadable recording uses some of these techniques in combination with my vast experience of driving tuition and knowledge of the driving test.

As well as starting and running the driving school I was also the initiator and proprietor of ADI Services (Driving School Suppliers) and as such am known to many instructors throughout the UK. During this period I produced and sold the first version of this book and accompanying recording which proved to work extremely well.

As you can imagine I was very busy, but now am retired (although still comparatively young) and have since had the time to re-write and re-record a greatly improved and refined version of the original work.

If you're serious about learning to drive but lack confidence or keep failing the test for whatever reason, the techniques and information herein will help you. But of course you must use them regularly as directed.

In order to gain a UK driving licence you have to pass the theory test, the hazard perception test and the practical driving test. You will also be expected to have a very basic knowledge of what's under the bonnet. Similar but varying regulations occur throughout the civilized world.

But wherever you live the practical test is without doubt the most difficult part to pass and that is mainly what this book and freely downloadable recordings are about.

The Practical Test

Despite every effort by the DSA (Driving Standards Agency) and no doubt all other agencies worldwide, the practical driving test is grossly unfair and will always be so. How easy or difficult your test will be is determined by the following, all of which you can either control or do something about:

- Your driving ability;

- Your country of residence;

- The test centre and area;

- The date and time of day;

- The test route;

- Traffic situations that you may encounter;

- The weather;

- The examiner;

- How you feel on the day;

- Your instructor and car;

- Your spouse, partner and friends / workmates;

- Previous tests;

- Your age;

- How much you enjoy driving;

- Your need to pass the test;

- Your parents and your childhood;

- Your attitude and confidence;

- The Zen of driving.

You are no doubt wondering how all of these things could possibly affect one isolated incident in your life. And furthermore how you can possibly control all of them or counteract any negative influences that they may have caused. But believe me you can and easily. Read on to see how!

Your driving ability

There are two main parts to driving: *'controlling ability'* - being able to put the vehicle wherever you want to and *'road procedure'* - knowing where to put it! The latter includes: having a good knowledge of the Highway Code; awareness of other road users; anticipation of potential hazards; good reactions and concentration etc.

The majority of driving books deal mainly with *'road procedure'* and as such are only applicable in the country they are written for.

This book doesn't specifically deal with *'road procedure'* and as such *is* applicable worldwide.

With regards to *'controlling ability'*, there is only one way of becoming adequate and that is - *'practice'* plus the correct *'theoretical knowledge'*. This obviously means driving lessons or private practice with a friend or relative etc. (if this is legally possible in your country of residence). The correct *'theoretical knowledge'* (with regards to *'control'*) will be dealt with herein.

But it's essentially important that you get the right type of practice. You will benefit practically nothing from driving along a straight road in fourth gear even for several hours. You need junctions, roundabouts and lots of stops and starts etc., but only according to your ability.

The best practice that you're likely to get is with your instructor, but at least you can be sure that it will be the right type of practice. The majority of my pupils had no other practice than with me.

In my opinion two *separate* hours per week or more with a good instructor (plus the information in this book) is the best way to learn. If you live a long way from the test area, you will occasionally need to take two hours together in order to get to and from the area. Taking your lessons in separate hours ensures that you have less time to *'forget'* between lessons and plenty of time to *'reflect'*. It also means that if you're *'having a bad day'* it will only last for one hour!

During the essential *'reflection'* periods between lessons you'd be surprised at how much you learn, a great deal of which is *'unconscious'*, more so with the information herein.

But of course not everyone can afford two lessons a week. Where I worked in Sheffield, many of the areas were very depressed and people simply didn't have the money. Therefore the majority of my pupils only took one lesson a week, which although not ideal can work as long as you are regular. If you do miss a lesson, try and make up for it by having two the following week. Less than one lesson a week only works in exceptional cases, but is basically a waste of time and money.

Avoid gimmicky *'intensive'* courses (i.e. learn to drive in a week etc.), they rarely work and even when they do they usually work out much more costly. These would also deprive you of the valuable *'reflection'* periods in between lessons which are vitally important. You simply wouldn't have the time to *'absorb'* the information before the next session begins.

While learning *'controlling ability'* you will automatically be gaining *'road procedure'* experience. In the initial stages it appears that gaining the *'control'* is by far the hardest. But although road procedure takes no physical effort, it is ongoing - there is always more to learn. You will soon learn that driving is far more of a mental activity than a physical one.

You can and should learn road procedure to a certain extent by reading books; the Highway Code and the Driving Manual etc., but even after driving for over 50 years, I still occasionally see situations that have never occurred for me before.

What you really need is *'experience'*, but unfortunately this can't be taught. You gain it automatically over a long time. This is why a 70-year-old driver with 50 years experience (but possibly failing reactions) will often react much more quickly to a dangerous situation than a 19-year-old with only two years experience (even though his reactions may be 100%), because the older driver foresees the danger - through *experience!*

This incidentally is something that you have to be so very careful of if passing in an automatic. Because they are so easy to control, it's possible to pass within as few as 10 hours from scratch, but even though you may have passed the test, you would still be very, very inexperienced and consequently very vulnerable for quite some time.

The idea of the test is to make sure that you have basic controlling skills and enough knowledge to hopefully live long enough to gain the experience that you really need. As well as helping you pass the test, the information herein and the accompanying recording will also help keep you safe.

Before attempting to take the practical test, you need to be confident that you can control your vehicle adequately even in difficult situations and have a sound knowledge of the Highway Code. Your instructor will tell you when you are ready for the test, but you should have a pretty good idea yourself as well. If you don't feel confident, the chances are that you're not ready.

Detailed information about controls and how to use them can be found in my book 'Clutch Control and Gears Explained', but less extensive details are also included later on in *this* book.

Your Country of Residence

The driving tests around the world vary enormously, but tend to be more difficult in the more economically advanced countries. Mexico is one of the easiest as you don't need to take a test at all, but unsurprisingly the accident rate is shockingly high.

The test in Pakistan is stupidly easy where there's an 80% pass rate and again a very high accident rate.

South Africa surprisingly has one of the most difficult tests, with a very low pass rate, but a very high bribery rate!

But most of the EU, the US, Canada, Japan and Australia have fairly stringent tests, with Finland being one of the most difficult, but also probably the best.

The age at which you can apply for a license and begin lessons, varies vastly from country to country and even state to state in the US. But it's normally between 16 and 18 years of age.

The Test Centre and Area

The DSA in the UK makes every effort to ensure that each test is conducted fairly and equally, but to be honest they're fighting a losing battle. They have absolutely no chance of making each test equally fair as there are too many *'variables'* involved, many of which will be dealt with as we go on.

But firstly, each test centre throughout the UK (and no doubt also worldwide) has a vastly different *'pass rate'*. Obviously these rates vary each year, but not by a great deal. The average UK *'pass rate'* nationwide is about 44%. But in the densely populated areas such as Birmingham or London it can be lower than 30%, whereas in the lesser populated areas such as remote areas in Scotland the *'pass rate'* can be higher than 75% or even 80%.

Clearly *some* of the candidates who fail in busy areas could be far more competent drivers than *some* who pass in less populated areas. How can this be fair?

Also, in the large cities where there are several test centres there can often be significant differences between each of them. When I was working in Sheffield there were three: Middlewood Road, Handsworth and Manor. They were all extremely different. Middlewood Road for instance had much more congestion and a lot more hills than the other two. Whereas Handsworth had some very fast roads and *'hairy'* roundabouts. Clearly the different areas were suited to different styles of driving. If you were good at *'clutch control'*, but didn't like driving fast or dealing with roundabouts - Middlewood Road might be the easiest for you. Whereas, if you were confident at *'getting your foot down'*, but didn't like congestion or *'clutch control'* - Handsworth might suit you better.

Manor was a mix of the two, but more interesting from an instructors point of view.

The DSA correctly say that there is more to learning to drive than learning a test route and ask that prospective candidates stay away from the test areas until just before the test. While I agree that the majority of training, especially in the initial stages (and always the parking and reversing exercises) should be undertaken away from the test areas, in my opinion it's essential that you are very familiar with the main junctions within the area. But you must take care not to interfere with any of the tests, or upset local inhabitants.

For instance in the Handsworth area of Sheffield there are some very complicated junctions joining the 'Parkway' dual carriageway, which to be honest, I doubt if any inexperienced driver (qualified or not) would get right first time.

Even with my vast experience, I'm not ashamed to tell you that I have made mistakes when driving in unfamiliar towns and countries which would have made me fail a test - partly through me being unfamiliar with the area, partly because of inadequate markings or signs and occasionally through my own stupidity. Even the best driving test examiner in the world (if he or she could be identified) at some time makes mistakes - it's human nature. Anyone who says otherwise is grossly mistaken, or lying.

The Date and Time of Day

The time of day most certainly has a bearing on your test. I'm not saying that one time is necessarily any better than another (as there are other variables to take into account), but it is a factor.

There's no doubt about it that certain situations are more likely to happen at certain times of the day. For instance, 8:30 in the morning in the UK can be an horrendous time, as you have the rush hour; the school run; lollipop people; delivery vehicles; as well as bin men on certain days etc.

Another factor is that there are often no waiting or stopping areas between particular times, often 8:00 - 10:30 am and 4:30 - 6:30 pm. This means there could be less parked cars to deal with, but more traffic. But at the tail end of these periods, you will have less of either, so this could then work to your advantage!

If you work during normal working hours it's likely that most of your lessons will be in the evenings or the weekends, which means that you will miss out on the school traffic and the delivery vans / lorries etc. Be aware of this and try and get some daytime weekday practice when you can, (when you have a day off etc.) it will surely help you.

Through my experience I can assure you that the very best time to take lessons in the UK is on a Saturday morning. You won't get school or rush hour traffic, but you will get lots of shopping traffic and pedestrians running out all over the place, but without too much congestion.

I found that the very worst time was 5:00 - 6:00pm, as everyone was just in a rush to get home and it was basically a waste of time due to the congestion. I used to go home for tea at this time and resume at 6:00pm which was much calmer.

As far as the test is concerned, the only time that I would specifically avoid is the first test in the morning or on a date when there is a particular event taking place in the area - important football match etc. I've usually found Christmas-eve to be quite a good day as the examiners are often in a good mood (which I know shouldn't have an effect, but sometimes does) and most of the shopping has already been done!

Another thing to consider is that if you're going to spend all day worrying about the test, a *morning* time might be better for you.

The Test Route

The route that you are taken on obviously has a bearing on the outcome of your test and on the surface it appears that this is out of your control, but I assure you it's not - more of this later.

Some routes are considerably more difficult than others, but of course you never know what is around any corner.

Many learners have an intense fear of busy roundabouts and would love to take a test without encountering these. At Middlewood Road Sheffield there is only one busy roundabout and one dual carriageway. Some of the routes don't go near either and can consequently be potentially much easier (although the DSA would never admit it).

I've no doubt that there are routes at remote test centres which are pathetically easy, with only the most basic of roundabouts (if any) and few traffic lights, difficult junctions or more importantly - traffic / pedestrians etc.

Traffic Situations that you may encounter

It's quite possible to have a potentially difficult route where you encounter virtually no difficult situations and vice versa - a really easy route where everything appears to be against you. No doubt most people would consider this to be luck - but I assure you it's not. There is no such thing as good or bad luck - I'll explain later.

I remember one extreme case when a woman pupil of mine took a test the day after Boxing Day at 9:00am at Handsworth Sheffield. This particular year it happened to be a Friday and 95% of the population were in bed, as hardly anyone else was working. The result was that she didn't encounter another moving vehicle for the duration of the test - the roads were empty. As she managed to control the vehicle adequately and made the required observations - she passed. The examiner just laughed! To be honest she wasn't particularly good and as Handsworth can be quite a vicious area, I doubt if she would have passed a few hours later. But it wasn't luck!

Over the years I've seen literally hundreds of situations where candidates who I know have been well good enough to pass have failed, often through *apparently* being victims of circumstance, and others who have passed who perhaps shouldn't have. With the information in this book and on the accompanying recording you will learn how to effortlessly put the odds firmly in *your* favour!

The Weather

Clearly the weather can have a bearing on your test. It's obviously far more comfortable to drive when the weather is pleasant - unless you're being dazzled by sunlight. It's also a fact that there is always more traffic when it's raining, as people who might do otherwise are less likely to walk.

In the event of rain or fog your windows will mist up and you must know how to deal with this as well as using the correct lights for the conditions.

In extreme weather conditions i.e. snow, ice or bad fog, your test would be cancelled and an alternative date arranged. Sometimes if it's borderline (particularly with fog) you may be given the choice, but informed that you mustn't blame the weather if you fail.

You think you can't control the weather? Now you probably really think I'm mad. Read on!

The Examiner

According to the DSA (in the UK) all tests are conducted the same - but they're not. All examiners (worldwide) are different as are all instructors. They may well have been trained to the same standards but they're *all* individual.

Fairly late in my career the DSA started keeping data on all instructors with regards to their test results - in order to identify any repeated failings which could suggest that the instructor may be at fault. At the same time I kept data on all the examiners who conducted my tests for the same reason. It became clear that certain examiners were more concerned about particular faults (as are instructors); although it has to be said that most examiners (and instructors) would pick up on the same serious or dangerous faults. But with the less serious ones there were big variations and as you can now fail on an accumulation of these, this could certainly mean that you could get a different result with a different examiner!

In the colour spectrum at *exactly* what point does blue become green? And in the taste spectrum at *exactly* what point does sweet become sour? And who decides? And at *exactly* what point is it incorrect to proceed at an amber traffic light? Within a fraction of a second this could be judged differently by different examiners (or by anyone) and this could make the difference between passing and failing a driving test.

This point alone is one of the reasons that the driving test can *never* be *'fair'* however much the DSA (or any other government body worldwide) may try to make it so! But I don't dispute that they are making an attempt at it.

The DSA would no doubt deny this and insist that all the examiners are trained to the same rigorous standards which may well be the case and I wouldn't argue with this, but this can't and doesn't take away the *'human factor'* which exists in all of us and thankfully even them - most of them anyway!

Obviously the examiner's manner and attitude will also have an influence on your test. It's to the examiners benefit as well as yours that you are feeling calm and at ease and most of them will try their best to bring this about. But if you feel that they have not conducted the test fairly, you would have a right to complain. However, the result of the test could never be altered (in the UK anyway); the best you could hope for is a re-test.

There was one examiner at Middlewood Road Sheffield who had a nasty habit of turning the air con off as soon as he got into the car (because he didn't like it). This resulted in one of my pupils having a re-test. The examiner has no right to touch any of the controls except to avoid an accident. You should ensure that the ventilation etc. is how YOU want it (as long as the windows are clear and the correct lights are on). However you must remember that the examiner is entitled to a certain level of comfort. If you have all the windows wide open and the heater blowing cold in the winter, he would have a right to terminate the test.

You've no doubt heard the myth that examiners are only allowed to pass so many candidates each month. This is complete nonsense despite your next door neighbour assuring you otherwise!

How You Feel on the Day

If you feel good, you're more likely to drive well. Make sure that you wear clothes and more importantly *'shoes'* that you're comfortable and familiar with. Don't get dressed up like you're going to church. Be casual and comfortable.

On the day of your test you will have a pre test lesson (which is one of the most important lessons that you will have). Take some time to relax before your instructor arrives. If you meditate, this would be a good time for it. If you smoke, it wouldn't be a good time to give up.

Make sure that you arrive at the test centre with plenty of time to spare (at least 15 minutes before the test). Most test centres have toilet facilities. If yours doesn't, make sure you know where the nearest one is!

Also try and get a good night's sleep the night before and try not to worry about it. I know this is easier to say than do but we'll discuss this more later.

Your Instructor and Car

Choose your instructor carefully. It's best to get one who comes personally recommended.

Many people will tell you that you get *'what you pay for'* - implying that the most expensive are the best. This may be the case with some things, but driving tuition isn't one of them.

Surprisingly the larger more expensive schools often have the least experienced instructors. Many of them are newly qualified or even trainees. In most cases these schools are nothing more than *'training grounds'* for instructors. They may work there for a few years after qualifying and then often move on to work for themselves. This of course is not always the case, but certainly more often than not. I can say this with no fear of recrimination, because it is the truth!

It also has to be said that *some* inexperienced instructors and even trainees are excellent, so be guided by how you feel. A fully qualified UK instructor will have a green octagonal badge in the windscreen, whereas a trainee will have a red triangular one.

The correct car for your size and build is also vitally important. Make sure that you can reach all the controls comfortably and have good all round vision. If you are used to it, a car with AC will be more comfortable. You need to be happy with both your car AND your instructor, if either aren't right - change them. Also make sure that your instructor guarantees to supply you with the car that you've been learning in for your test. Not a similar one but the same one (again the large schools often fail here).

There are occasions when a vehicle breaks down or needs replacing, just before your test. In this event a decent reliable instructor / school will give you some free time in the replacement vehicle or pay for another test date for you. Again it does happen that the vehicle breaks down during your test. In this event (which is no-one's fault) the test will be abandoned and your instructor *should* pay for an alternative appointment.

Your Parents and your Childhood

Most people start learning to drive from a very early age albeit unconsciously. I was born at a time when little boys played in pedal cars / soap box carts, while little girls played with dolls and prams. Men were expected to be the breadwinners (and drivers). And a woman's place was at home with the kids, cleaning and cooking - but certainly not driving! Please don't think I'm sexist, I'm simply stating facts!

Beano character Dennis the Menace used to get a good pasting at the end of every comic strip. Now this is considered *'inappropriate'*, so the little bastard gets away virtually *'Scot free'!* But actually he's not as bad as he used to be! Noddy and Big Ears used to share a bed perfectly innocently and no-one was concerned. A few years later this become *'inappropriate'* so they were given separate beds. I haven't seen it lately, but they're probably back in one bed now with PC Plod thrown in for good measure! And perhaps I shouldn't even mention the naughty Golly who was later replaced by a Bear due to fears of racism, although at the time this was certainly never the case. Golly's were loved and cherished by all my generation - I still have mine!

Clearly there is no *'right'* or *'wrong'* (although you may think there is), but the *'opinions'* of the time are deeply programmed into our minds, which change from generation to generation. What you *'think'* is probably not *'your'* opinion at all.

If, by accident of birth you were born a Muslim or a Hindu or a Jew etc., the chances are that you would remain so all your life and rigorously defend *'your'* views or opinions despite the fact that they were never really *'your'* views or opinions at all!

Do you think that any of the following childhood events helped me pass my driving test four months after my 17th birthday?

- Doing *'three point turns'* in my pedal car from *'year dot';*

- Taking great interest in how my father used to drive;

- Being generally interested in cars from a very early age;

- Reading the Highway Code from an early age;

- Taking pride in passing my cycling proficiency test at school;

- Growing up with the *'expectancy'* that I would be a good driver;

- Driving off road with my father's guidance from age 12 whenever I could;

- Taking my first (on road) driving lesson on my 17th birthday;

- Being given much encouragement from my father who was the eighth person ever to pass the Institute of Advanced Motorists test.

Despite all of the above I still managed to fail my first test. But it must have helped me learn quickly and comparatively easily. In retrospect, I am now glad that I failed my first test, as it gave me the valuable experience of how crap it feels.

Women of my generation generally had a horrendous time learning, partly due to the following reasons:

- Women drivers were considered to be a joke;

- It was generally accepted that driving was a *'man'* thing;

- Very few were interested in driving;

- As children very few had pedal cars or soap box carts;

- As children less had bicycles;

- Few were given any encouragement to learn;

- Many were told: 'Don't be stupid you'll never do it etc!'

- Those who did learn usually left it until they were older.

If all of this is true, which it is, is it any wonder that *in those days* women had much more difficulty?

Reluctantly I have to admit that in some respects women make better drivers than men. And as this is a proven fact, prior to 2013 their motor insurance premiums were often a lower price. But unfortunately this was seen to be sexist and the government ended it in the UK, resulting in increased premiums for everyone - such is the result of government meddling!

Generally speaking (but by no means always), men are more skilful than women (hence the shortage of women **F1** drivers), but the typical accident that a male is likely to be involved in would be a high speed overtaking one causing huge damage and possibly loss of life. Whereas the typical female accident would be reversing into a gate post! Hence the insurance statistics!

Another factor that often makes women safer drivers than men is that many have a natural ability to *'let go'* if another motorist upsets them. Whereas we males have an inbuilt *'need'* for revenge, which is sometimes difficult to ignore even for the most experienced! Being overtaken is a threat to one's manhood!

Clearly men and women are wired up differently, each having their own strengths and weaknesses - it's probably something to do with the Mars and Venus thing!

Young women of this day and age usually make ideal pupils and learn very quickly because:

- They are young enough to get the *'control'* easily;

- They are mature enough to simply follow their instructors advice;

- They probably *did* have a pedal car or cycle as a child;

- Most now have a genuine liking for driving;

- Most *believe* that they will be successful;

- They usually don't have any of the early childhood negative *'conditioning'* mentioned previously.

Can you imagine how difficult it would be to learn if as a child you were brought up in the jungle and consequently had never seen a road, let alone a car or traffic lights or spoke any comprehensible language etc.? The whole process would be completely alien to you and learning would be a total nightmare. Before you even began the normal process of learning to drive, you'd have to become familiar with the environment that we all take for granted - i.e. roads, footpaths, roundabouts, traffic lights etc.

Of course the above example is a little extreme, but some immigrants have enormous difficulty due to their past. I can tell you for a fact that teaching first and second generation Asian immigrants (and please don't take this as *'racist'* remark) was not easy to say the least, despite the language barrier. Whereas the third and fourth generations who are of driving age now, have far less difficulty.

I've no doubt that many UK instructors are now struggling with first and second generation Somali immigrants. Again please don't take this as being racist in any way, I'm simply stating facts.

Your Spouse / Partner and Friends / Workmates

It's a sad fact that some men don't want their wives / partners to be successful for various reasons. Some will see it as a threat to their manhood or think that they'll lose the family car. Others may fear the new independence that their partner may gain when they pass.

If this is the case with you, you will be fighting against all sorts of pressures and negativity. I've seen this on numerous occasions.

You'll have to put up with snide sarcastic comments like: 'Haven't you passed yet?' 'When I did it I only had six lessons and passed first time!' etc. The truth is that they probably had an awful lot more than six lessons and the driving test and road conditions have changed out of all recognition over the last few decades, so a comparable is impossible.

Number one rule that I used to tell all my pupils was: 'don't tell anyone (apart from your instructor) when you are taking your driving test'. If you do you'll find that:

- You will be given all sorts of useless advice;
- You may have the *'Mickey'* taken out of you; and
- You'll have numerous *'good luck'* messages that you don't need.

All of these create added pressures. Before and during the test you'll be thinking about all the people that you've got to phone afterwards etc., instead of thinking about what you are doing now! So you'll end up taking the test for them instead of for YOU.

If you can get away with it, it's not a bad idea to keep the fact that you are *'learning'* a secret from as many people as possible. Just arrive with the pass certificate one day and surprise them.

Previous Tests

A previous test (or tests) can have a negative effect on you, as you will often have a bad memory of it / them which can influence the present. This effect can be neutralised or reversed by implanting positive *'memories'* or *'suggestions'*. Using the information herein will do this automatically for you.

Your Age

From the point of view of *'controlling ability'*, unfortunately age does come into it. There's no doubt about it that the under 30's find it a lot easier (male & female). But if because of age or some other reason you have immense difficulty with clutch control etc., then you would be wise to consider an automatic.

You may find that various individuals will try and talk you out of automatics. All the horrors that you may hear about them are mainly myths. It is true that they are a usually a little more expensive if buying from new and they do use a little more fuel (5 - 10%). Also if you have a flat battery, you cannot bump start them - but so what? Always carry some jump leads with you and don't leave your lights switched on unnecessarily when you're parked!

From a learners point of view, it can cut the amount of lessons required in half or less, mainly due to the fact that you don't need to learn *'clutch control'* and *'stalling'* is impossible.

The downside is that if you pass in an automatic in Europe, you will not be eligible to drive a manual without taking a further test. But unless you want to become a professional driver (in a lorry or bus etc.) who cares? After gaining experience in an automatic, passing in a manual later would be much easier, if you really wanted to.

Ironically, you could pass your test in the US in an *automatic* and then come to the UK and legally drive a *manual* vehicle on the left hand side of the road. But to be honest I wouldn't recommend it if you've never driven one before!

I personally prefer automatics now, simply because I think they're more pleasurable - especially in traffic jams. You can tuck your left foot away and forget about it.

Having said all this, I have taught many people in their 60's in manuals. But each year more and more vehicles are coming onto the road, which makes learning progressively more difficult (particularly in manuals).

If you're over forty and want to learn quickly, do yourself a favour and go automatic - you'll not regret it. But the last section of this book *does* give quite a bit of information for learning in manuals.

How Much You Enjoy Driving

You can't be forced to like driving and if you don't - why do it? If you're being forced into learning for whatever reason you will probably pack it in or at least it will take much longer. Usually the more you enjoy driving the quicker you will learn.

On numerous occasions I've had the job of teaching people where someone else is paying. This is rarely a good idea unless the learner is genuinely committed.

I used to dread the occasions where a husband bought driving lessons for his spouse as a *'surprise'*. If they genuinely wanted to learn, it was a nice surprise, but on numerous occasions they were terrified and refused to get in, which apart from anything else was a waste of *MY* time.

Your Need to Pass the Test

Similar to the above, if you're leaning to drive only because of *'work'* pressures etc., unless you genuinely want to do it, it's going to be more difficult and cost you more.

Your Attitude and Confidence

If you consider it carefully, you'll probably agree that a combination of the factors mentioned so far must influence your ability to learn and the time that it will take you. But even if all of these are *'positive'* your *'attitude and confidence'* could still let you down.

You could be the most wonderful learner driver in the world, but if you've got the wrong attitude you'll fail the test. I've seen this happen on numerous occasions and can guarantee to you that all other experienced instructors have too. I know it to be true.

It's possible and often happens that a person is outwardly confident but inwardly negative and vice versa. I don't doubt that everyone is nervous on a driving test, but the problem goes way, way beyond *'nerves'*.

You might find this difficult to believe, but somehow YOU create the *'right'* or *'wrong'* conditions for your test. This is the reason why some people apparently have an easy test and others don't. There is no such thing as LUCK! There's also no such thing as an IDLE THOUGHT!

- YOU determine which examiner you have, what mood he / she's in and what route you're taken on;

- YOU determine how much traffic will be on that route and in exactly what position;

- YOU determine how difficult it is to enter a roundabout, or what colour the traffic lights will be;

- YOU determine what the weather is like on the day of your test

- YOU determine the amount of idiot pedestrians who walk out in front of you on your test;

- YOU determine where the bin lorry will be etc., etc.

WHILE EVER YOU THINK / BELIEVE THAT YOU WON'T PASS THE TEST - YOU'RE RIGHT - YOU WON'T! - BUT YOU COULD CHANGE YOUR MIND!

Basically you get everything that you *'ask'* for! Outwardly I'm sure that you want to pass the test, but if you spend hours worrying about it, you are in fact inwardly *'praying'* for failure. And it's the *'inwardly'* bit that matters most! But don't worry, we can fix it. This is what the techniques described later are really all about. All I ask is that you have enough faith in me to try it then you can prove it to yourself.

Sometimes exactly the right attitude is created accidentally.

Following are a few case histories:

Case 1

Was a young woman with average ability. On the day of her test she seemed to be in a dream and wasn't taking much notice of me at all. She had a lousy pre test lesson (which is usually a good sign). Anyway, she passed, but even then showed no emotion at all. On the way home after many minutes of silence, she told me that one of her brothers had just drowned - ironically the third one who had drowned in the same place in the Irish Sea.

I know it's a bit extreme and impossible to replicate, but as a result of this she subconsciously created exactly the right conditions for her test. Basically she couldn't care less whether she passed or failed, which released all the fear.

Case 2

Was a young man with way above average ability. He'd been driving illegally for years, so without making any judgement on him, he was very experienced. He'd only had about four lessons with me, just enough to *'dot the i's and cross the t's'*.

Basically he had the ability to *'walk it'*. But on the test as he was coming up to a difficult uphill junction to turn right, a lorry cut the corner in front of him. Immediate emergency action was required (which I'm sure he took), but the examiner took action as well (not realising that the candidate could have been quick enough), which caused failure. You could say that he was a *'victim of circumstance'*, but I know different.

Sadly, unconsciously he was expecting the test to be much harder than it really was - and consequently made sure that it was! Even sadder, he didn't take another test. He went back to his illegal ways, yet with only a tiny bit more effort he could have been legal.

Case 3

Was a young woman with average ability who had failed two tests. On the previous attempts she had worried furiously beforehand, however on the last attempt she was due to go for an important job interview later the same day which she was even more worried about for some reason. The result was that she passed the driving test and loused up the interview.

Whereas on the previous attempts she created the wrong conditions through worrying too much, finally, she had something else to take over the worry.

Case 4

Was a 69 year old lady, who'd been learning for about five years. To be honest, she was as good as she was going to get. On a good day, she could get it right, but she was far from *'consistent'*.

This was her thirteenth test. Before the test she was driving appallingly. I felt really bad, as this time I thought that she'd got no chance and was feeling guilty about all the money I'd taken off her. She also realised how bad she'd driven on the pre test lesson and had *resigned* herself to failing yet again, but decided to go through the motions anyway. The result was that she finally passed.

But there was a big difference to her previous attempts. She'd *surrendered* to *'what will be will be'* which is the best attitude. The majority of people often blow the whole thing way out of proportion which creates the wrong conditions.

Case 5

Was a 60 year old lady who was incredibly nervous. When she first came to me I had just finished the fore runner of the accompanying recording and she was the first person to use it. Fortunately, she really believed in it and used it every day. She learned easily and passed first time. The whole process was *'plain sailing'*.

Case 6

Was a *'dotty'* young woman with average ability, she also used the recording regularly and on her test she went up the kerb while reversing (which would normally be a failing point), but the examiner said 'Don't worry, no women can reverse anyway' and passed her! I've no doubt that the DSA would deny this but I also know that it happened!

Creating the Right Attitude

Desperate money rarely wins! If you are in the situation where you think that you *have* to do it, you probably won't. The best way is to just take it as it comes and see what happens. Try not to expect to pass or fail - just do it. When taking the driving test, the best thing to be concentrating on is *'driving the car'* (believe it or not!), not trying to figure out what the examiner is thinking / doing. You can only think of one thing at once, just think about (and concentrate on) what you are doing NOW!

Most people take the test far too seriously. Try and develop that *'whatever will be will be'* attitude. I know probably more than most that this is far easier to say than do, but the following techniques and / or recording WILL solve the problem completely and easily.

Don't take my word for it - prove it for yourself!

The Zen of Driving

Many years ago when the IAM (Institute of Advanced Motorists) first came into being, a major part of their test was the *'running commentary'*, where the candidate was required to give a commentary of his / her thoughts. Sadly this was dropped from the test over 40 years ago.

You could either simply use driving as a means of transport or you could turn it into an enjoyable *'art form'* or even a conscious *'self awareness meditation'*.

This can be achieved by totally absorbing yourself in the process and by doing so you will become a *superb* and very aware driver. And this is what you should be going on in your head whilst driving - especially on the test!

Constantly think: - Vision; Speed; Position!

Remember - the *vision and road conditions* determine the *speed*, the *speed* determines the *gear!*

Vision

- What's ahead of me? - Pedestrians; cyclists; children; animals; other motorists; potholes; obstructions; traffic lights; pedestrian crossings; gradients; junctions etc.;

- What's behind me? - Does someone want to over take me?

- What's coming towards me - how fast are they approaching and do I need to take any action?

- What's to either side of me? - Has something that was behind me vanished that could be in my blind spot?

- What blind areas are there? - Shop doorways; parked cars; blind corners; restricted vision due to other vehicles etc.;

- What is the extent of my vision?

- How far can I see ahead before my vision is obstructed by bends / hills etc.?

- What road signs / markings are there?

- Am I clearly visible to other road users and are my intentions clear? - Use correct lights and signals for the conditions and horn if necessary.

Speed / Gears

- What's the speed limit?

- Am I travelling at the correct speed for the road and traffic conditions and vision?

- Am I in the correct gear for the speed, conditions and gradient?

Position

- Am I in the correct position?

- Will I shortly need to change position?

- Is the position of another vehicle suggesting that they might be about to change course?

As you familiarize yourself with this practice you'll find that the process can become mind bogglingly complicated as more and more simultaneous events occur. This is why even a good experienced driver often has to drop out of a conversation to put full concentration / attention on the situation being dealt with. And is also one of the reasons why mobile phones / satnavs and sometimes even radios can become dangerous distractions. Yet frequently inexperienced drivers think that they can drive safely with the radio blaring at intolerable volumes and a mobile phone glued to their ear! Well all I can say is that they must know something that I don't! And if you think I'm a grumpy old git you're probably right! - *It's evolutionary!*

One rule that has kept me safe is - only ever drive at a speed so that you can stop safely well within the distance that you can see to be clear having regard for the road and traffic conditions!

Finally never forget that **every** parked car is a potential serious accident, because of doors opening or children running out from blind areas or the vehicles moving off without warning etc! So either give enough clearance to deal with the situation easily or reduce speed so that you can stop - or a combination of both.

And remember - that child may be deaf!

The Vast Power of Your Mind

The Bible tells us that we all can move mountains should we so wish, simply through the power of our *'word'!* - Most people believe that this is complete nonsense, and if this is what you firmly *believe* - you right it is! - But what if it's not?

You Reap What You Sow!

You reap what you sow! This is also mentioned in the Bible as well as numerous self help books.

You wouldn't plant carrot seeds if you want to grow onions would you? And having decided to grow onions, you'd then (presumably) plant them carefully in fertile soil and water them regularly. It's blatantly obvious!

And in case you haven't worked it out yet, the same applies to everything else. Every *'thing'* in existence began as a *'thought'* or *'seed'* and was materialised as a result of correct nurturing i.e.:

- first the *'thought'* - with the result *seen* or *visualised* as occurring NOW in the present moment - the *'seed'*:

- then the *'re-enforcement'* - pinpointed attention and belief - *'the fertile soil'*;

- then the *'repetition'* - *'regular tending and watering'*.

This is how everything is created - be it a *'thing'*, *'work of art'*, *'piece of music'* or *'situation'* etc. And it's also how you pass or fail your driving test!

You may be thinking what a load of cobblers all this is, but while I'm writing it I'm thinking how unimportant passing the driving test is and how the information and techniques given here can be (and should be) used for far more important purposes. The only reason that I'm bothering is because I have a vast knowledge of both driving and mind techniques and I've put the two together to help YOU!

I also strongly urge you to use the same techniques in any other areas of your life that need altering or improving.

The Universal Subjective / Subconscious Mind

You are in direct and constant communication with every*body* and every*thing* in existence - whether you like it or not. As well as having an individual subconscious mind, we are all connected to the same Universal Subjective mind which is why and how we (mainly unconsciously through our personal subconscious) *'use'* (but not *'control'*) other people to create situations that we want (or don't want depending on how we use them).

All your thoughts, wishes, fears and especially your *'spoken word'* are reflected into the Universal Subconscious and then channelled out in different directions to bring about your conscious experience. And this is all achieved without any conscious effort of any kind.

Even every material *'thing'* is a thought materialised. <u>You</u> can bring into being any *'thing'* or *'situation'* that you really want.

YOU CAN

IF YOU THINK

YOU CAN!

The Law of Reversed Effort

The more you consciously try to *'resist'* anything - the more it will *'persist'*.

Could you walk along a plank 20' (6m) long by 3' (1m) wide if it was suspended approximately 2' off the ground? Of course you could - anyone could - easy peasy! Now what if it was suspended across a 200' deep ravine full of hungry crocodiles? Now you probably couldn't - I know I couldn't, but why? Because in the first example you'd see no problem and just do it, whereas in the second you and me both would be *'focussed'* on falling off and being eaten by crocodiles.

This is often the case with the driving test and why you can drive perfectly OK with your instructor, but go to pieces when the examiner gets in. If you *'focus'* on failing - that's exactly what YOU will bring about. If you *focus on your driving* instead of passing or failing, you will increase your chances of bringing about the favoured result.

For a statement / suggestion to bring about the required outcome this is also why it should be worded in a *'positive'* way, i.e.: *'I will not be afraid of the driving test'* could have the opposite effect because the subconscious only picks up on the phrase *'afraid of the driving test'* and disregards the *'I will not be'*! It's also incorrect because it refers to a future time (which never actually arrives) rather than the present (which is the only time in which anything actually occurs). A better statement might be: *'On the driving test I am confident, relaxed and alert, and am able to deal with all situations correctly and skilfully as they arise'.*

IF YOU THINK YOU CAN'T YOU'RE RIGHT!

Your Word is Power

Every word that we hear, speak or think has some power. Listening to, speaking or even thinking apparently innocent statements such as the following over a period of time could affect you accordingly (for *'good'* or for *'bad'*):

- I'm always *tired*;

- He / she / you / it *will be the death of me*;

- My feet are *killing me*;

- I could *die* for a cup of tea / cigarette;

- I'm starving / freezing / boiling etc.;

- It *always rains* on Bank Holidays / on my driving test etc.;

- I'll *never win* the lottery / be rich / pass the driving test etc.;

- However much I diet I still *can't lose weight*;

- I can eat what I want and never put on an ounce;

- I can't control my nerves on my driving test / at interviews etc.;

- Even hypnosis can't make me give up smoking;

- I'm *too old* to: learn to drive / go to Australia / learn music etc., etc.;

- This country is *getting worse* each year;

- I'm *sick with worry;*

- I'd give *an arm or a leg* to have - *whatever;*

- Nothing is as good as it used to be etc., etc.

Be extremely careful about what you say and think, as ultimately you will get 100% of what you ask for! IF YOU DON'T WANT 'IT' - DON'T SAY 'IT' OR SEE 'IT', OR HEAR 'IT' OR EVEN THINK 'IT'! Remember the *'Three Wise Monkeys'!*

Spend a little while noticing how much of this rot you hear from friends / family etc., and also how much *'garbage'* you tell yourself through your *'inner chatter'*. The first step is being aware of it. You will eventually learn how to control it.

Not happy with what you've got? Learn to ask for something different!

You want immediate proof? - Try this!

Next time you are out looking for a parking space (this works just as well for passengers as for drivers) say to yourself that there *is* a space exactly where you want it. If you can, try and visualize it. Don't worry if it doesn't work first time, keep doing it - you'll soon be amazed!

This works for me 99% of the time. At first I thought it was spooky, but now I know that it's nothing more than a natural *'law'*. Of course if you're convinced that it won't work - you're right - it won't - but it will be the same law giving you exactly *what you ask for!*

We often go to Matlock Bath (an inland resort in Derbyshire) and have parked in the *same free space* at very busy times regularly for over 30 years - coincidence? - could be, but I don't think so!

You use this same method to *'cause'* every event in your life but mainly unconsciously. Looking back at my own life I now realise how I've caused many events which I've both wanted and not wanted to occur. Now that I know how it works I am more able to control it (not yet perfectly, but getting there).

In 2006 using this method we managed to sell our villa in Cyprus and the small business that I started out there and our car to three different individuals ALL to coincide EXACTLY with the flights that we'd booked back to the UK *six months previously* - coincidence? No way! - I planned it and worked on it for at least 30 minutes a day during that six month period.

YOUR WORD IS POWER

USE IT WISELY!

There's been many other *'coincidences'* like this for me both before and since. I could fill a book with them - and will do sometime.

How conscious are you?

Probably 85% - 90% of the time you are unconscious of what you are doing. This is not meant to be an insult - it's a fact!

Most of us can only consciously think of one thing a once, but almost constantly we need to perform numerous tasks simultaneously, most of which are done *'unconsciously'*, i.e. breathing, walking, digesting, swimming, DRIVING etc.

Ask any experienced driver EXACTLY what he / she does during the last 3 seconds of the approach to a difficult uphill left hand junction. Unless they're a driving instructor they will tell you incorrectly (even though they will probably actually do it correctly).

Most will say that they look both ways, assess the situation and proceed if safe. This is what they are *'conscious'* of, but they will also:

- Regulate the last part of the approach speed;
- Depress the clutch pedal;
- Probably turn half a turn to the left (to follow the kerb);
- Select first gear;
- Partially engage the clutch at the same time as setting the engine revs at the correct level to gain clutch control;

- Continue turning at the same time as making observations and using clutch control as necessary.

And they will also be digesting their last meal, breathing, taking care of all the other internal bodily requirements as well as probably having a conversation at the same time!

One of the reasons that learning anything is difficult at first is because it has to be learnt *'consciously'* before it can become *'unconscious'* and consequently automatic. In the case of driving, trying to be conscious of all of the above as well as making the correct assessment / observations etc. is mind bogglingly difficult. But once the *'controlling'* part has been thoroughly learnt (through repetitive practice) and has become automatic, the conscious mind only has to deal with the apparently more important *'road procedure'* - assessing the situation etc.

So clearly the *'unconscious'* mind has its uses. In fact we couldn't function without it. But if we become *'conscious'* of what we are allowing in there, *we* end up in control!

Belief

Whatever you firmly believe - *is!*

Just before we left Cyprus, a good friend of mine was talking to me about *'Crystals'*. She was / is convinced of their beneficial properties.

Although I am certainly into most things *'mystical'* I am also aware that there is a lot of nonsense out there that unscrupulous

ANYTHING IS POSSIBLE

IF YOU BELIEVE!

individuals are making a fortune out of. Please don't misunderstand me I'm certainly not necessarily saying that *'Crystals'* is one of them. I really don't know, and would have to study the subject carefully before reaching a proper conclusion.

Anyway off the top of my head and without really thinking I said to my friend that I thought it was all a load of cobblers! But her reply to me hit me like a sledge hammer. She said: 'Yes but if you BELIEVE in them they really work!'

This is so true. And true of anything. The power is not necessarily in the things in which you believe in but in the BELIEF itself! This is why lucky charms work for some people and not for others. Whatever you firmly believe - positive or negative, good or bad - IS! My friend later gave me some crystals to keep me safe, which I shall cherish as I believe that SHE has put power into them through her belief!

Personally I have a great belief in pyramids and tetrahedrons. I really don't know whether it's these shapes which help me or simply my belief in them. But they work for me!

Technique 1

Firstly I assure you that this technique **will work**. Of this I am 100% sure. But you must take the small amount of effort to prove it to yourself.

How quickly it will work will depend on your present level of negativity. 20 years of wrong thinking isn't going to be neutralized in one or two sessions - or maybe it is - but generally speaking the more often you do it the quicker it will work.

Just before falling asleep and just as you wake, you are in a natural state of hypnosis. These states are called *'hypnogogic'* and *'hypnopompic'* and are particularly good times to use this technique, but any other time will work also.

Further on in this book you will find a list of declarations / affirmations. These can be used in this first technique as well as featuring subliminally, audibly and bilaterally in the second (audio) technique. If you haven't already done so, print these out and keep them separate.

CHANGE YOUR MIND

TO CHANGE YOUR WORLD!

Remember that these were written with over 30 years of instructing experience, over 50 years of driving experience and over 45 years study of various *'mind techniques'* so you can be pretty sure that they are correct. However, if for some reason you object to any of them, please do not use them.

You may notice that all the suggestions are in a positive form and in the present tense for the reasons stated previously. It's very important that they are not altered in any way.

'I WILL BE' is like an unplanted seed which cannot materialise - nothing more than a *'wish'!*

'I AM' is like a seed correctly planted which MUST materialise. It's a Universal Law!

'I AM THAT I AM' - as God said to Moses!

Step by step

1. Make some time for yourself when you will not be disturbed for about half an hour. Turn your mobile phone off and shut yourself in a quiet room.

2. Choose a few of the declarations that feel right for you (no more than 5).

3. Sit or lie down in a comfortable position and relax as best you can. Taking a few deep breaths will help you do this.

4. To get yourself in the right frame of mind, think of something relaxing like a clear starlit night or a view across a calm lake etc. Or think of a time when you felt deeply relaxed and content. Really try and feel it as best you can. Bringing EMOTION into the equation helps tremendously.

5. Read the chosen declarations EXACTLY as they are written, preferably out loud (but at least verbalised). Repeat each one a few times. If you can, try and visualise the reality of what you are saying. Using a mirror and looking into your eyes will enhance the process.

6. In between each declaration, just sit and relax for a minute or so.

7. Finish the session with a feeling that what you have stated is true and is a reality now - even though it isn't!

8. Choose one of the declarations (that appeals to you most), write it on a card, keep it with you at all times and read it (out loud or verbalised) as often as you can think of it in between sessions. Applying small coloured self adhesive sticky dots around your environment can be used as an effective reminder, or maybe set an hourly alarm on your phone!

That's it - simple! So simple that you probably don't believe a word of it!

Don't confuse this with *'Will Power'* or *'Positive Thinking'* etc.; this is far more powerful and incredibly easy. And don't think you can't do this - you've been doing it all your life. This is just a refined version - a way of planting the seeds correctly! If you think about it carefully, it's even logical - just like planting vegetable seeds! AND IT WORKS!

The more you repeat these statements / declarations to yourself the sooner they will be accepted by your subconscious mind and the sooner they will become a reality for you. Once the subconscious accepts a statement it will act on it whether you like it or not! Don't worry if you feel like you are lying to yourself - just do it! The more you do it, the more you'll believe it - the stronger the belief - the sooner it will happen. Real strong *'Belief'* produces miracles.

In-between sessions also try and become aware of your *'inner chatter'* and exactly what YOU are saying to YOU! As soon as you notice any negative nonsense, put a stop to it immediately. It's very likely that your subconscious will fight back in the initial stages by telling you that this is complete nonsense. And of course if you think it's nonsense - you're right - it is! - But you could change your mind!

Technique 2

If you use the first technique as directed (which is incredibly powerful), you will not need this second one. However you may want to use it additionally.

For this technique you will need to download the audio mp3 recording at http://martinwoodward.net/driving_dl.html . If you wish you can burn this onto a CD, however in order to maintain the quality please only record from my original. On this link there is also a free bonus *'confidence'* mp3 which you may also like to use. This too uses Binaural Beats.

If you have any problems with the download contact me via the contacts page of my website and I'll sort it out for you.

The main recording consists of:

- Subliminal, Audible & Bilateral Suggestions;
- Binaural Beats;
- Natural Sounds / Tibetan Bells;
- Breathing Rhythm.

Subliminal, Audible & Bilateral Suggestions

Many of the declarations (as listed later) are included but spoken in the second person (you rather than I). They are initially recorded so that they can only be heard *'subliminally'*. This means that they are just below the level of your conscious awareness, but can be heard by your subconscious. This is recognised as a very powerful technique for influencing the subconscious. Don't attempt to listen for them consciously - believe me they are there. I spent hours recording them and making sure that the level is as it should be!

As the session progresses the volume of the suggestions fades up so that they are fully audible and mostly bilateral which means you will hear a different suggestion in each ear which *'tricks'* the subconscious to accept them. However by the time this occurs you may be in such a relaxed state that you'll barely hear them anyway. Don't try and listen for them and don't try not to. Just relax.

Binaural Beats

This is a method which can automatically and effortlessly put you into a relaxed state in order for the suggestions to have a powerful effect on your subconscious mind.

Binaural Beats are achieved by playing two very slightly different frequencies (one in each ear via stereo head / ear phones). The brain then creates the *'imaginary'* binaural beat which can be clearly heard. For example if the frequency of 100Hz is heard in the left ear and 110Hz in the right ear, the *'ghost'* binaural beat of 10Hz will result.

The closer the two frequencies are together, the slower the beat will be and the deeper the level of relaxation that will result.

Throughout the day and night your brainwaves naturally vibrate at varying frequencies ranging from1.5Hz - 40Hz in the following scale:

Beta	15Hz	-	40Hz	-	Normal Waking Consciousness
Alpha	9Hz	-	14Hz	-	Light to Deep Relaxation
Theta	5Hz	-	8Hz	-	Deep Relaxation - Meditation
Delta	1.5Hz	-	4Hz	-	Deep Sleep - Total Unconsciousness

If the brainwaves drop to zero - you'd be brain dead! But don't worry this couldn't happen. There is in fact no Binaural Beat which could achieve this as at zero the two frequencies would be the same and therefore no binaural beat would be produced!

When listening to binaural beats, your brainwaves will gradual *'attune'* to the binaural frequency which causes the temporary alterations in consciousness.

In the *'alpha'* state the mind is relatively open to outside suggestion and consequently this is the level which the recording will take you to in order for the suggestions to have the required effect.

The recording is 60 minutes in length and will start off in *'beta'* 20Hz (normal waking consciousness), will gradually assist you down into the *'alpha'* state 10 - 12Hz and then gradually back to *'low beta'* 15Hz at the end of the session.

The beats are clearly audible, but very much in the background, so don't try and listen for them - they are there!

Should you become disturbed while in the *'alpha'* state, you may feel a bit groggy (like you've just woken up), and may need a few minutes to re-adjust, but this is nothing that is going to cause you any problems.

The more you use the technique the easier you will fall into the *'alpha'* state and consequently the more benefit you will receive.

Please don't think that there is anything unnatural about these states. In certain situations you could be in the *'alpha'* and even *'theta'* states when fully conscious. For instance; when relaxed and walking through the woods etc.

More details of Binaural Beats, clearly audible beat samples and recordings descending to deeper levels can be found in my website at: http://deep-relaxation.co.uk .

Natural Sounds / Tibetan Bells

These are nothing more than background noises to help bore your conscious mind into relaxation. However you will find them deeply relaxing and comfortable to listen to.

Breathing Rhythm

This again is just a pleasant sound mask which you can follow or not as you choose.

Step by Step

1. Make some time for yourself when you will not be disturbed for at least an hour. Turn all your phones off and shut yourself in a quiet room. Ideally this should not be within an hour after eating (as your digestive system will make it difficult for you to relax);

2. Sit or lie down in a comfortable position, close your eyes and relax as best you can. Taking a few deep breaths will help you do this. As with the first technique to get into a good frame of mind - think of a relaxing scene etc.;

3. Using stereo ear / headphones, listen to the recording at a comfortable volume. If you don't have any ear / headphones - buy some - even cheap ones will do. Please remember that Binaural Beats will only work in stereo;

4. Following the breathing rhythm (to a count of about 8 if you inhale and exhale at the same rate or to an inhale count

of 12 and let the exhale find its own way out) will help you into a fairly deep state quickly and effortlessly - or you can simply ignore it;

5. As the recording ends in low beta, this recording could also be used at night as you fall asleep, in which case you'll awaken normally.

At the end of the session, give yourself some time to *'come round'*. As a precaution I suggest that you leave at least 30 minutes before doing anything potentially dangerous - climbing a ladder or feeding your pet crocodile etc.

So surely this is simply hypnosis?

I agree that there are similarities in the fact that positive suggestions are implanted into the subconscious mind, but it's not the same for the following reasons:

- There is no hypnotic induction or verbal wake up section. But if you use the *'hypnopompic'* or *'hypnogogic'* periods just before falling asleep or just as you wake up the process will be far more natural;

- The powerful binaural beats will assist the relaxation process to a remarkable degree;

- The powerful subliminal and bilateral suggestions are rarely used in hypnosis;

- *You are in complete control* at all times and can get up and walk away any time that you choose - but you probably won't want to due to the deep feelings of relaxation that the process induces;

- You are free to read all of the suggestions that are on the recording (as shown further on) and if you choose to reject these - simply don't use the recording.

Are Binaural Beats / Isochronic Tones safe?

For most individuals binaural / monaural beats and isochronic tones are perfectly safe as they are non addictive and non abusive. However they may not be suitable for a small percentage of the population as indicated here:

- Epilepsy or other seizure sufferers. Due to the effect that the repeating sound pulses may have on the brainwaves, similar to strobe lighting, they could possibly induce a seizure and should therefore be avoided.

- Due to the fact that their brains are still developing, they are not recommended for use by children except under strict medical supervision.

- Anyone who uses a pacemaker or is taking medication (legal or otherwise), should only use brainwave entrainment recordings with medical advice.

If you don't fall into one of the above categories, there's no reason why they can't be used safely and effectively, but of course if you have any negative effects, simply stop using them. If you are in any doubt seek professional medical advice.

Due to the feelings of relaxation they will induce they should never be used when driving, cycling, cooking, operating machinery or when engaged in any other activity that may put you in danger.

Declarations / Suggestions

Some of the following suggestions / declarations are repeated throughout the recording in technique 2. A selection of these should also be used in technique 1. Do not alter the wording in any way.

I could have made thousands of these, but in order to keep things simple AND effective I have carefully chosen these.

General

- When driving I am always calm, relaxed confident and alert.

- I can see myself as a safe motorist who is knowledgeable, skilful and courteous to all other road users.

- I can see myself driving the car of my dreams and handling it safely and skilfully.

- I allow myself to enjoy driving both on the open road and in busy congested traffic.

- When driving I allow myself to be calm, relaxed and comfortable yet acutely aware.

- I enjoy driving smoothly, courteously and economically. My passengers always feel safe and comfortable when I am driving.

Driving Test

- On the driving test I am confident, relaxed, comfortable and alert. I am able to deal with all situations correctly and skilfully as they arise.

- I can see myself passing the driving test now. I can see the examiner handing me the pass certificate. I can feel the excitement of passing now.

- I can see myself passing the driving test with confidence and ease.

- I allow myself to pass the driving test with confidence and ease.

Highway Code

- I am thoroughly familiar with every aspect of the Highway Code and follow its advice rigorously.

- I observe, understand and take appropriate action of all road traffic signs and road markings.

Reversing

- I can reverse any vehicle safely, confidently and skilfully in all situations and always remember to observe the front and sides of the vehicle as well as the rear.

Mirrors

- I use the mirrors correctly and effectively before every change in speed or direction or before signalling.

- I always make full effective use of my mirrors well before changing speed or direction or before signalling.

- I am continually aware of all following traffic and take the correct, appropriate action as necessary.

Speed

- I have superb judgement of speed and distance and use it effectively whilst driving.

- I drive at a speed so that I can always stop safely well within the distance that I can see to be clear, taking into account road, traffic and weather conditions.

- I am capable of stopping my vehicle under full control quickly and safely in all emergency situations.

Anticipation

- I am constantly aware of the blind spots on both sides of my vehicle and take the correct and appropriate action when moving off, changing lanes and leaving roundabouts etc.

- I approach all green traffic lights in preparation for stopping until I reach a point when I know that it's correct and safe to proceed even if the lights change to amber.

- When driving I always look well ahead and *'read'* the road. I take the correct and appropriate action skilfully and confidently.

- I react to all situations quickly, correctly and confidently with regard for all other road users.

Pedestrian Crossings

- I approach all pedestrian crossings cautiously and am aware of all blind areas.

Roundabouts / Junctions

- I am capable of dealing with even the busiest of roundabouts safely, correctly and confidently.

- When emerging at junctions I always double check for cyclists and / or motorcyclist who could be hidden from my view by whatever reason.

Obstructions

- When passing parked vehicles or other obstructions, I am aware of all possible eventualities and allow the appropriate clearance or reduce speed accordingly.

Ability Analysis Test

This section consists of a number of questions and answers designed to help you understand *how* to control a manual gearbox vehicle (*'stick shift'* to those of you the other side of the pond). As it is concerned only with *'control'* it is perfectly applicable to every country in the world (left or right hand drive), as controlling a manual vehicle is the same everywhere. **Furthermore this information can never become out of date** - not while we have manual vehicles anyway!

If you only intend driving an automatic, most of this section will be irrelevant to you, although an understanding of gears is still useful.

Please don't think that this bears any resemblance to the UK *'theory test'* - this is completely different and not comparable in any way.

Neither is it designed whereby you keep a score of your correct answers and congratulate yourself if you score over a certain percentage. **Nothing less than a 100% understanding is acceptable.**

To help you gain a complete understanding the answers have been given directly after the questions.

Unlike many *'road procedure'* questions; you will find that *anyone* who is able to drive a *manual vehicle* will know the answers to *all* of these questions (perhaps after a little thought) otherwise they simply wouldn't be able to drive one.

It therefore follows that if you *don't* know the answers to these questions, you will *not* be able to drive one - hence their importance!

Some of the questions have more than one possible correct answer and sometimes, you are not offered a choice of answers, but are just *given* the correct one to save confusion.

There are no *'trick'* questions; they are all geared towards helping you understand completely and quickly. So anyone struggling to learn a manual (*'stick shift'*) will learn much more quickly with this information.

To use this section effectively, mark the questions that you don't understand and keep coming back to them - eventually you *will* understand - *I promise!*

The Clutch

Q 1

What is the clutch and what is it used for?

A 1

The clutch pedal *operates* the clutch, which is a device which enables us to either connect or disconnect the engine from the drive wheels either totally or partially and is used for moving off, changing gear, and stopping - *and clutch control - which is a combination of moving off and stopping.*

The clutch in its very simplest form consists of two circular plates - *about the size of tea plates.* One of these plates is connected to the engine and the other is connected to the gearbox. When the clutch pedal is up these plates are held firmly together by high pressure springs and the clutch is *engaged.* When the clutch pedal is down the plates are separated and the clutch is then *disengaged.*

The diagram here shows these two conditions.

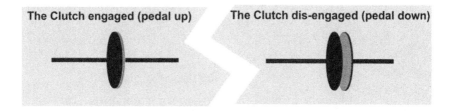

The Clutch engaged (pedal up)   **The Clutch dis-engaged (pedal down)**

Q 2

On a front wheel drive vehicle the engine connects to:

   a) The front wheels?

   b) The rear wheels?

   c) All four wheels?

A 2

The front wheels.

Q 3

On a rear wheel drive vehicle the engine connects to:

   a) The front wheels?

   b) The rear wheels?

   c) All four wheels?

A 3

The rear wheels.

Q 4

On a four wheel drive vehicle the engine connects to:

a) The front wheels?

b) The rear wheels?

c) All four wheels?

A 4

All four wheels - some 4x4 vehicles are permanently four wheel drive, others have the option to be two wheel drive.

Q 5

Are front wheel drives any easier or more difficult to drive than rear wheel drives or four wheel drives for a novice driver in normal conditions?

a) Yes?

b) No?

A 5

No. They are driven exactly the same and a novice would not notice the difference in normal conditions. However front wheel drives (and 4x4's) can be considerably better in snow due to the weight of the engine over the drive / steering wheels.

Q 6

If the engine is turning, what will happen if you attempt to move the gear lever without depressing the clutch pedal?

a) Nothing out of the ordinary?

b) This could cause extreme damage to the gearbox?

A 6

This could cause extreme and expensive damage to the gearbox as well as possibly making the vehicle shoot forwards (or backwards) suddenly and out of control.

What you would in fact be doing would be joining a *moving* cog (gear) to a *stationary* one as shown in the diagram below. Clearly this could result in the teeth flying off in every direction!

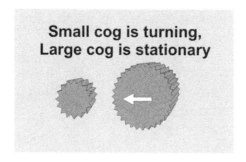

To avoid damage, both cogs (gears) must be either stationary or moving at the same speed so that they can intermesh correctly and easily.

Q 7

When the clutch pedal is *up* and the gear lever is *in neutral* - is the engine connected to the drive wheels?

    a) Yes?

    b) No?

    c) Partially?

A 7

No. This can be seen in the following diagram. In this condition the engine can be safely started. Notice also that with the engine running, both clutch plates and the top gear cog would be turning at the engine speed, as they are all connected. Whereas the lower gear cog, drive shaft and rear wheels are not connected to the engine and are therefore stationary (or freewheeling if the vehicle is coasting).

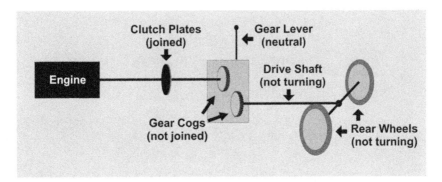

Q 8

When the clutch pedal is *down* and the gear lever is *in neutral* - is the engine connected to the drive wheels?

   a) Yes?

   b) No?

   c) Partially?

A 8

No. Similar to the last question, but in this case only the front clutch plate would be turning and everything else along the line would not be connected to the engine and therefore stationary (unless the vehicle is coasting).

In this condition there are two splits in the *transmission* circuit - one between the engine and gearbox and one between the gearbox and drive wheels.

Consequently it would be perfectly safe to move the gear lever without fear of anything horrible happening as neither cog (gear) is turning. This is shown in the next diagram below.

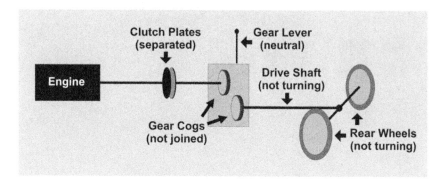

Q 9

When the clutch pedal is *down* and the vehicle is *in gear* - is the engine connected to the drive wheels?

    a) Yes?

    b) No?

    c) Partially?

A 9

No. This is the next position in the moving off process. The vehicle is *in gear*, but as the clutch pedal is depressed there is no join between the engine and the gearbox - hence the engine is *not* connected to the drive wheels.

The next diagram shows this condition and the fact that the front clutch plate is joined to and turning with the *engine* whereas the rear plate is joined to the *road* and would only be turning if the vehicle was freewheeling - *as it would be during a moving gear change.*

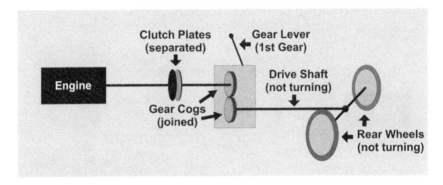

A close up view of *neutral* as against a *gear selected* is shown below.

Q 10

When the clutch pedal is *down* and the vehicle is *in gear* - is the gear:

    a) Selected?

    b) Engaged?

A 10

In this condition the gear is *selected* as it is not joined to the engine (as in the last *transmission* diagram above). It becomes *engaged* when the clutch plates join - *pedal up.*

Q 11

When the clutch pedal is *down,* is the engine connected to the gearbox regardless of which gear it's in?

a) Yes?

b) No?

c) Partially?

A 11

No. Depressing the clutch pedal separates the engine from the gearbox as shown in the last *transmission* diagram.

Q 12

When the clutch pedal is *at 'biting point'* (also referred to as *'point of control'* or *'point of contact'*) and the vehicle is *'in gear'* - is the engine connected to the drive wheels?

a) Yes?

b) No?

c) Partially?

A 12

It's partially connected - not enough to make the vehicle move forwards, but enough to prevent it from rolling backwards. In this condition the clutch plates are slipping and will burn out if held for too long - *ideally 5 seconds should be the maximum*. This is the next step in the *uphill start* procedure and is used to prevent the vehicle from rolling backwards when the handbrake (or parking brake) is released. See the next diagram.

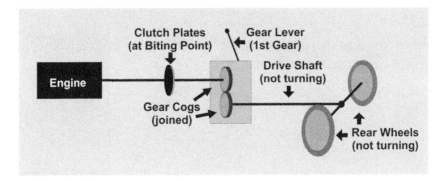

Q 13

When the clutch pedal is *up* and the vehicle is *in gear* - is the engine connected to the drive wheels?

a) Yes?

b) No?

c) Partially?

A 13

Yes. This is the condition that the vehicle will be in when driving along and is shown here (below) in first gear, but is the same in any gear - everything is connected, therefore the vehicle must be moving assuming all four wheels are on the ground.

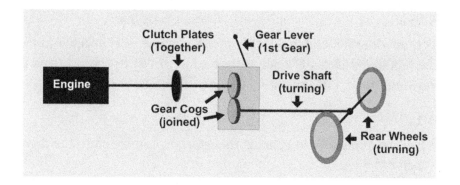

Q 14

When the clutch pedal is *up* and the vehicle is *in gear* - is the gear:

a) Selected?

b) Engaged?

A 14

In this condition the gear is *engaged* - as in the last diagram. Remember the gear is engaged when the clutch pedal it *up* and is *selected* when the clutch pedal is *down*.

Q 15

When the clutch pedal is *up*, is the engine connected to the gearbox regardless of which gear it's in?

a) Yes?

b) No?

c) Partially?

A 15

Yes, anytime the clutch pedal is *up,* the engine is connected to the gearbox, regardless of which gear it's in or even in neutral. This is shown in the last diagram (and the first *transmission* diagram).

Q 16

When the vehicle is *in gear,* is the *gearbox* connected to the drive wheels?

a) Yes?

b) No?

c) Partially?

A 16

Yes, the gearbox is connected to the drive wheels in this condition as shown in the last three *transmission* diagrams.

Q 17

Assuming all four wheels are on the ground; when the clutch pedal is *up* and the vehicle is *in gear* - is the vehicle moving?

a) Yes?

b) No?

c) Not necessarily?

A 17

Yes it must be, as shown in the last diagram - assuming all the wheels are on the ground and the engine is running.

Q 18

Assuming all four wheels are on the ground; when the clutch pedal is *down* and the vehicle is *in gear* - is the vehicle moving?

    a) Yes?

    b) No?

    c) Not necessarily?

A 18

Not necessarily; if it is it will *not* be propelled by the engine and will be *coasting*. This in fact is the condition that it will be in *during* a gear change for the short length of time that the clutch is depressed (see 3rd *transmission* diagram).

Q 19

Assuming all four wheels are on the ground; when the clutch pedal is *up* and the vehicle is *in neutral* - is the vehicle moving?

    a) Yes?

    b) No?

    c) Not necessarily?

A 19

Not necessarily and certainly not normally. This is the condition shown in the first *transmission* diagram when you would normally start the engine. But the vehicle *could* move in this condition, but only by *freewheeling* down a hill. It will not be propelled by the engine. This is commonly known as *coasting*.

Q 20

Is coasting dangerous?

    a) Yes?

    b) No?

    c) Not necessarily?

A 20

Coasting can be extremely dangerous especially if attempted by the inexperienced as it *could* lead to loss of control of the vehicle. In the UK (and probably most other countries also) coasting would certainly result in failing the driving test.

Q 21

Does coasting save fuel?

    a) Yes?

    b) No?

    c) Not necessarily?

A 21

Of course coasting saves fuel and anyone who tells you otherwise is lying, but it's probably a false economy as it could easily lead to an accident.

Moving Off

Q 22

Before starting the engine you should ensure that:

a) The handbrake is applied and the gear lever is in neutral position.

b) The handbrake is applied and the gear lever is in first gear position.

c) The clutch pedal is depressed.

Which is correct?

A 22

In order to start the engine safely the engine must be disconnected from the drive wheels and the handbrake should be applied. This is achieved by ensuring that the gear lever is in neutral position (with handbrake applied) and then it would normally make no difference whether the clutch pedal is up or down.

However it is possible to safely start the engine with the gear lever *in gear* **as long as the clutch pedal is depressed** which disconnects the engine from the gearbox. This is particularly useful to save time after stalling, but if you don't understand this, never do it!

Note also that in order to start some modern vehicles, the clutch pedal must be depressed. This is in fact the case with my current car which is a Ssangyong Korando. Although this is becoming more common, right now it's the exception rather than the rule. But check your vehicle's handbook!

Q 23

What would happen if you started the engine in gear with the clutch pedal up?

a) It wouldn't start?

b) It would leap forwards?

c) It would start normally?

A 23

The vehicle would leap forwards out of control possibly causing damage to other vehicles or pedestrians, more so if the handbrake is not firmly applied.

This is possibly one of the reasons that some manufacturers are now making this eventuality an impossibility - as on my Korando!

Q 24

How do you move off on an *uphill* gradient?

A 24

After safely starting the engine and doing all the other necessary checks, proceed as follows:

1. Depress the clutch pedal fully (to the floor);

2. Select 1st gear;

3. Set the engine revs' (just the first change in engine tone from tick over) and keep it steady;

4. Allow the clutch pedal to come slowly up to the '*biting point*' - sometimes referred to as the '*point of control*' or '*point of contact*';

5. Keep both feet still;

6. Gently release the handbrake *or parking brake* and make any slight adjustments to the clutch if necessary to ensure that the vehicle *does* stands still;

7. Return your hand to the steering wheel and make forward, rear and blind spot observations, then *signal only if necessary;

8. When ready to move away, relax pressure on the clutch pedal a fraction, then _keep both feet still_ - the vehicle will move forwards;

9. After the vehicle has gathered momentum, remove your left foot from the clutch pedal and put it to the side;

10. Accelerate to increase speed and change up as necessary.

*Regulations regarding signalling before moving off can vary from country to country!

Q 25

What is the difference between an uphill start and a level start?

A 25

The only difference is that there is no fear of rolling backwards on the level; therefore the handbrake could be released before finding the _'biting point'_.

Q 26

When moving off uphill or level what is the most likely cause of stalling the engine?

a) Releasing the engine revs as the clutch comes up (two left feet syndrome)?

b) Not being gentle enough with the clutch pedal?

c) Selecting an incorrect gear (3rd instead of 1st)?

d) Releasing the handbrake too late?

A 26

Any of the above could cause the engine to stall.

Q 27

What will happen if too much acceleration *(gas)* is used when moving off uphill or level?

a) The engine will *'roar'*?

b) The vehicle will possibly move off too quickly?

c) Clutch damage could result?

A 27

All or any could occur.

Q 28

What is the cause of the vehicle rolling backwards when moving off uphill?

a) Not allowing the clutch up far enough before the handbrake is released?

b) Attempting to move off without the vehicle being properly *in gear?*

A 28

Either or both could be the cause. Make sure that you push the gear level far enough to select the gear correctly and always release the handbrake slowly being ready to re-apply it if necessary!

Q 29

Could the vehicle move off with the handbrake still applied?

    a) Yes?

    b) No?

A 29

Yes, but if the handbrake is applied firmly the vehicle will stall, if not it will move off but obviously will be restricted and could eventually burn out the brake linings.

Q 30

After stalling on an uphill gradient, why is it that sometimes the vehicle rolls backwards and sometimes it doesn't?

A 30

This is very important so make sure that you understand this.

After stalling on a gradient, if the clutch pedal remains up and the vehicle is in first gear, the compression of the engine (even though it's not running) *could* prevent the vehicle from rolling backwards, but the moment you depress the clutch pedal, this will release this compression and cause the vehicle to *instantly* roll with the gradient.

This is why as soon as you stall; the first thing that you must do is *secure* the vehicle (by applying the hand brake) *then* depress the clutch pedal before restarting the engine.

This incidentally is why the vehicle should be left *in gear* when parked on a hill *(1st if uphill, reverse if downhill)*, to make the vehicle more secure should the handbrake fail. This creates a similar condition to *'park'* in an automatic. But don't rely on this 100% as it can still move when the engine cools down, so as an additional precaution the wheels should be turned into the kerb.

Q 31

How do you move off on a downhill gradient?

A 31

The correct procedure is as follows:

1. Depress the clutch pedal fully *to the floor;*

2. Select 1st or 2nd gear depending on how steep the gradient is - *steeper gradients will require 2nd gear;*

3. Depress the footbrake with the right foot;

4. Release the handbrake;

5. Return your hand to the steering wheel and make forward, rear and blind spot observations, then signal only if necessary;

6. When ready to move away, simply release the footbrake and the vehicle will of course move forwards at a speed determined by the gradient;

7. Gently allow the clutch pedal right up before hardly any speed has gathered then remove your left foot from the clutch pedal and put it to the side;

8. Increase speed and change up as necessary.

Q 32

What will happen if I attempt an uphill start on a downhill gradient?

A 32

It will still move away, but you will not have both hands on the steering wheel which could cause loss of control, particularly if moving off at an angle.

Q 33

Is it possible to stall the engine when moving off downhill?

    a) Yes?

    b) No?

A 33

Yes, it's still possible, but less likely. The only way that this could occur would be if you allowed the clutch pedal up too soon - the vehicle needs to be moving first!

Stopping

Q 34

Which gear should you stop in?

    a) 1st?

    b) 2nd?

    c) 5th?

A 34

You can stop the vehicle in any gear.

Q 35

What is the correct procedure for stopping?

A 35

The correct procedure for stopping is as follows:

1. Use the mirror(s) and warn any other road users or pedestrians of your intentions if necessary;

2. Reduce speed by releasing the accelerator and / or applying the footbrake progressively (how much of which will be determined by your speed and the gradient);

3. Depress the clutch pedal just before the vehicle comes to a halt and at the same time relax pressure on the footbrake so that little or no pressure is applied at the point of stopping;

4. Apply the handbrake (or parking brake) and put the gear lever back into neutral position *before* moving your feet;

5. Remove your feet, or move off again as necessary.

Q 36

So which pedal goes down first the clutch or the footbrake?

a) The clutch?

b) The footbrake?

A 36

It could be either depending on which is needed first which is dependent on the speed and the gradient. The faster the vehicle is travelling the earlier the footbrake will be needed, but the clutch pedal is depressed *just* before the vehicle comes to a halt (to prevent the engine from stalling). The two pedals are not connected.

Q 37

What will happen if the clutch pedal is depressed too soon?

    a) The engine will stall?

    b) Speed will increase?

    c) Nothing?

A 37

Being too early depressing the clutch pedal could cause an *increase* in speed due to the engine braking being release too early. This could be disastrous in an emergency situation, in which case you'd be better off being too late with the clutch and stalling the engine!

Q 38

What will happen if the clutch pedal is depressed too late when stopping?

    a) The engine will stall?

    b) Speed will increase?

    c) Nothing?

A 38

The engine will judder and / or stall, but (as just stated) is the lesser of the two evils in an emergency.

Q 39

What will happen if the footbrake is applied too fiercely when stopping?

a) The vehicle will stop sooner?

b) The vehicle could skid out of control?

c) The vehicle will jerk to a halt?

A 39

Being too heavy on the footbrake will cause a jerky halt at best or skidding and total loss of control in extreme cases. Braking should always be firm if necessary but *progressive*. Be particularly careful on bad road surfaces (wet, snow, gravel, wet leaves etc.).

The following two graphs show examples of correct and incorrect braking from 70 mph. The first one (where full braking pressure is applied and maintained) would certainly result in a skid (and total loss of control) even on a good dry road surface.

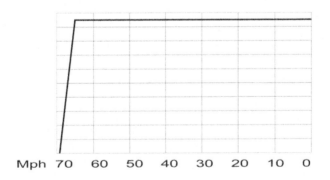

The second graph below shows a controlled progressive stop where braking pressure is released to nil at the point of stopping.

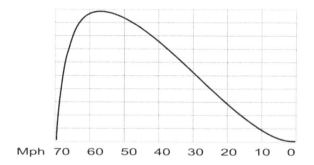

Mph 70 60 50 40 30 20 10 0

Extra care should be taken with the footbrake in any conditions other than a smooth dry road surface.

Q 40

Which foot is used to operate the footbrake on a manual vehicle?

    a) The right foot?

    b) The left foot?

    c) Either foot?

A 40

The *right* foot, as the left foot will be needed at the same time to operate the clutch pedal. The *only* time *ever* that the left foot should be used on the footbrake (on a manual vehicle) is after driving through a flood where it can be used *briefly* to dry the brake linings (with your right foot on the accelerator).

Clutch Control

Q 41

What is clutch control?

A 41

Clutch control is a method used to move the vehicle slower than it will normally go in 1st or reverse gears.

Q 42

Clutch control can be used:

a) Uphill?

b) Downhill?

c) Level?

Which are correct?

A 42

Clutch control can be used on the level and uphill gradients only - *not downhill.*

Q 43

In which situations are you most likely to need clutch control?

A 43

Clutch control is mainly used when in the following situations:

- Creeping forwards to gain vision at junctions etc.;
- Moving slowly in traffic jams;
- Parking (in forward and / or reverse gears);
- Turning the vehicle around using forward and reverse gears;
- Moving off at an angle.

The following diagram shows a vehicle moving off at an angle where it is necessary to move very slowly at the same time as turning the steering wheel.

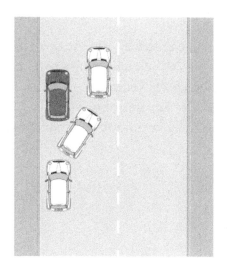

Q 44

Is it possible to drive a manual car without using clutch control?

    a) Yes?

    b) No?

    c) Possibly?

A 44

No.

Q 45

So what technique is used instead of clutch control when moving very slowly downhill?

A 45

When needing to move extremely slowly on downhill gradients this is achieved by keeping the clutch pedal down and releasing and re-applying the footbrake as necessary - but as soon as speed is increased above an absolute crawling pace, the clutch must be fully engaged otherwise you would be coasting and possibly lose control.

Q 46

What is the correct procedure for using clutch control?

A 46

The procedure for using clutch control is as follows:

1. Follow the same procedure as the uphill or level start up to point 8 where the vehicle first begins to move forwards;

2. Before the vehicle gains momentum, re-apply pressure on the clutch pedal slightly which will make the vehicle stop again;

3. As the vehicle glides to a halt, relax pressure on the clutch pedal to allow the vehicle to move forwards again;

4. Repeat 2 & 3 as necessary until you are ready to either move away completely - *keep both feet still* or stop - *depress the clutch pedal.*

Q 47

So when using clutch control, the clutch is just the same as a brake then?

   a) Correct?

   b) Incorrect?

A 47

No, this is most definitely incorrect. The clutch is nothing like the brake. *Dipping* the clutch simply releases the drive from the engine allowing the gradient (or lack of drive) to slow the vehicle down. So if too much speed is gathered before *dipping the clutch,* it simply won't work. It only works at a crawling pace!

Q 48

When using clutch control will *dipping* the clutch further slow the vehicle down quicker?

   a) Yes?

   b) No?

A 48

No it won't, because it's the gradient that will be slowing the vehicle down. The steeper the uphill gradient is the quicker it will slow down!

Q 49

Is stalling the engine possible when using clutch control?

   a) Yes?

   b) No?

A 49

Yes, just the same as with moving off, if you release the accelerator (or don't keep it steady), or are not gentle enough with the clutch pedal the engine will stall.

Q 50

Can using clutch control excessively damage the vehicle?

    a) Yes?

    b) No?

A 50

Yes, using it for more than a few seconds could damage the clutch linings.

Q 51

If you smell burning when using clutch control what is this and what should you do about it?

A51

This will be the clutch linings burning caused through excessive revs or over use of clutch control. If this occurs you must let the clutch cool down by either stopping and switching off or driving off and avoiding using the clutch for several minutes.

Q 52

Are diesel engine vehicles any easier to control than petrol ones?

A 52

To an experienced driver it makes no difference, but to a novice, diesels are easier in the fact that less acceleration is needed to move off, so it is often possible to use clutch control with little or even no acceleration. This makes them *slightly* less likely to stall and *slightly* easier to control.

Gears

Q 53

Which is the most powerful forward gear?

    a) 1st gear?

    b) 2nd gear?

    c) 5th gear?

A 53

1st gear is the most powerful (and lowest) forward gear although reverse is generally more powerful.

Q 54

Which gear enables the vehicle to reach its fastest speed?

    a) 1st gear?

    b) 2nd gear?

    c) 5th gear?

A 54

5th gear (or 6th if there is one), although this is the least powerful, but remember *power* is not *speed*.

Q 55

So what actually happens in the gearbox when a different gear is selected?

A 55

The main *drive* cog (gear) is connected to a different sized cog (gear) which alters the speed that the wheels turn in relation to the engine. Neutral and 2nd gear selected are both shown in the next diagrams.

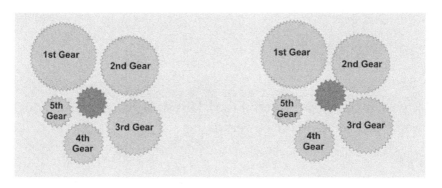

Q 56

At what speed should you change up from 1st to 2nd gear?

   a) 5mph?

   b) 10mph?

   c) 20mph?

A 56

All of the above answers are both correct and incorrect as it depends on the gradient and the gear ratio of the vehicle. As less power is required travelling downhill, you can change up sooner.

And as more power is required going uphill you need to gain more speed first.

Basically, as you *speed up you change up*, then as you *slow down* (and want to continue without stopping) *you change down*.

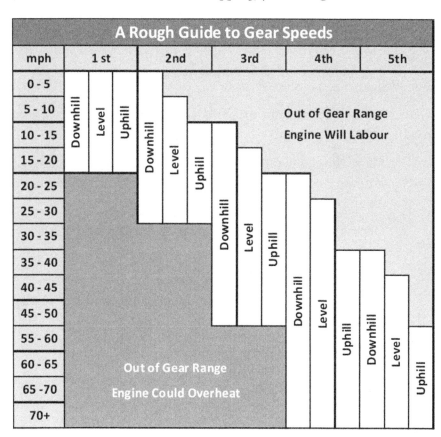

A Rough Guide to Gear Speeds

The preceding chart shows a *rough* guide on varying gradients. But remember that it is *only* a rough guide as different gradients and gear ratios can vary enormously.

Q 57

What is the correct technique for changing up when driving along?

A 57

The technique is as follows:

Gather the correct amount of speed (which is minimal on a level road);

1. Place your hand on the gear lever in preparation for moving it to the correct position taking into account the spring (see diagram below);

2. Depress the clutch pedal and release the accelerator *together;*

3. Gently move the gear lever into the appropriate position after which your hand must be immediately returned to the steering wheel;

4. Gently allow the clutch pedal back up to the top and remove your left foot completely and rest it to the side;

5. Accelerate (or brake) as necessary.

The diagram below shows the *most common* gear layout. Note that there will be a spring pushing the lever into the centre of the neutral position as shown by the black dot. So you will need to push against this spring to select 1st, 2nd and 5th gears.

To select reverse gear there will almost certainly be a safety *gate* to make it more difficult to select by mistake (when going forwards).

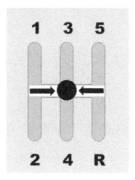

Although five gears is the most common, some vehicles have six gears, in which case this will be where reverse is in the above diagram, and reverse will then probably be to the left of first (through a safety gate).

Q 58

What will happen if you engage an incorrect gear?

A 58

The engine will labour, roar or stall.

Q 59

Why is it that sometimes the gear lever won't move easily?

A 59

If the gear lever will not move easily, it's because you are either pushing it in the wrong direction or not depressing the clutch pedal enough (it must be fully depressed to the floor).

Q 60

What will happen if you don't release the accelerator when depressing the clutch pedal (when changing gear)?

A 60

The engine will roar.

Q 61

Why is it that sometimes the gear grates when changing gear?

A 61

This is due to not having the clutch pedal fully depressed or allowing the clutch to partially engage before the gear is selected. This could cause expensive gearbox damage.

Q 62

What will happen if you are not fast enough changing gear?

A 62

If travelling uphill, for the length of time that the clutch is *disengaged* (depressed) the vehicle will be slowing down, so if you are not quick enough completing the process, you will need the gear that you've just changed out of! When travelling downhill, speed will *increase* during the gear change according to the gradient.

Q 63

Why is it that sometimes the vehicle jerks as the clutch is engaged?

A 63

This is generally due to the clutch not being engaged smoothly enough - practice makes perfect. Don't get too hung up on this just do your best! More information about making smooth gear changes can be found in my book 'Clutch Control and Gears Explained'.

Q 64

Is the technique for changing down, the same as for changing up?

A 64

The technique for changing down is basically the same as changing up, but very often when changing down you will also be slowing down and would therefore be using the footbrake at the same time.

The procedure for *changing down* is as follows:

1. Reduce speed if necessary by braking or releasing the accelerator;

2. Place your hand on the gear lever correctly positioned for the appropriate gear;

3. Depress the clutch pedal and release the accelerator *together* if you are using the accelerator, ___but___ if you are slowing down it's more likely that you will be using the footbrake in which case this *must not* be released;

4. Gently move the gear lever into the appropriate gear after which your hand must be immediately returned to the steering wheel;

5. Gently allow the clutch pedal back up to the top and remove your left foot completely and rest it to the side;

6. Accelerate or continue braking as necessary.

Note that at point 3, as the clutch is disengaged it's likely that there will be an *increase* in speed due to the engine braking being released, so you may even need to increase footbrake pressure *slightly* at this point.

Q 65

When slowing down, do you change down first or slow down first?

A 65

It's best for the vehicle *and normal* to slow down *then* change down, but in certain weather conditions it may be necessary to change down first.

Q 66

Is it possible to miss gears out?

    a) Yes?

    b) No?

    c) Only when changing down?

A 66

You can miss gears out when changing up *or* down as long as the speed and gradient is compatible for the gear (see previous chart). This is often referred to as block changing. The most common block change is 4th - 2nd. Others are: 5th - 3rd, 5th - 2nd, 3rd - 1st, 1st - 3rd, 2nd - 4th and 3rd - 5th.

Q 67

Having changed up through the gears, why will you need to change down?

a) After slowing down?

b) To ascend a hill?

c) To descend a hill?

d) To gain power to overtake another moving vehicle?

A 67

All of the above are correct. Basically, changing down gives you more *power*. It perhaps seems contradictory that you may need to change down both to *ascend* and *descend* a hill. But you are using the *power* in different ways. Ascending a hill you will obviously be using the power to physically get up the hill, but when *de*scending a hill you will be using the power to hold the vehicle back as *engine braking*.

Q 68

So which gear do you need to change into when going up a hill?

A 68

It depends how heavy your vehicle is, how powerful your engine is and how steep the hill is. See the following diagram.

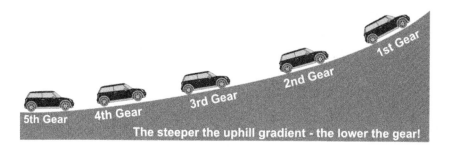

Q 69

So which gear do you need to change into when going down a hill?

A 69

This depends on how heavy your vehicle is, the road conditions and how steep the hill is. Sometimes a gear change will not be necessary at all.

Q 70

Can you change gear without depressing the clutch pedal?

A 70

Very experienced drivers can do so easily by correctly matching the engine and gear speeds, but most novice drivers attempting this are likely to cause extensive damage - so don't bother trying it!

-----oooooO0000Oooooo-----

Hopefully you've understood much of the above, but if not please keep re-reading what you don't understand and eventually you will.

Further information can be found in my book 'Clutch Control & Gears Explained' - which is similar but *far more in depth*. See: http://martinwoodward.net for details of this.

Thank You

Well, that's it folks! But last but not least I'd like to thank you sincerely for buying this book. It's been my sincere wish to provide more value in real terms than the cost of this book. I hope that you think that I've succeeded, if so your positive feedback at Amazon, iBooks, Kobo, Nook or Lulu etc., would very much be appreciated.

Please also remember that if you have any trouble with the downloads, I can be contacted at the contact pages of any of my websites listed on the next page and will be happy to help.

Kind Regards and thanks again,

Martin

Other Books by Martin Woodward

Clutch Control & Gears Explained

The New Drivers Handbook

Driving Instructor Training Exposed

See: http://martinwoodward.net for details of the above

Learn How to Play Electronic Keyboard / Piano in a Week! ♫

Keyboard Improvisation One Note at a Time ♫

Learn How to Play Piano / Keyboard for Absolute Beginners ♫

Learn How to Play Piano / Keyboard By Ear! ♫

Learn How to Play Piano / Keyboard With Filo & Pastry ♫

New Easy Original Piano / Keyboard Music Books 1 & 2 ♫

See: http://learn-keyboard.co.uk for details of the above

See: http://deep-relaxation.co.uk for details of items below:

The Golden Sphere - An Introduction to Rebirthing and A Course in Miracles

Brainwave Entrainment Plus ♫

Relaxation CD's & mp3 Recordings ♫